Leadership H.E.A.R.T. Unleashed

Leadership H.E.A.R.T. Unleashed
Igniting a Revolution of Influence and Impact

Chad L. Patterson

Published by Game Changer Publishing

Paperback ISBN: 978-1-961189-68-3
Hardcover ISBN: 978-1-961189-69-0
Digital: ISBN: 978-1-961189-70-6

GC GAME CHANGER
PUBLISHING
www.GameChangerPublishing.com

DEDICATION

This book is dedicated to my wife Liz, children, family, and my sister Julie
for loving and supporting me in the adventure called life!

Read This First

Just to say thanks for buying and reading my book, I would like to give you a free welcome call with me, no strings attached!

Leadership H.E.A.R.T. Unleashed

Igniting a Revolution of Influence and Impact

Chad L. Patterson

GAME CHANGER
PUBLISHING

www.GameChangerPublishing.com

Table of Contents

Introduction

Leadership affects everything. I believe this wholeheartedly. Do you? This book is built on this premise. If it is proven to be true, leaders at every level have a high calling in their lives to love, serve, and lead with excellence. For us to love, we must know love. For us to serve, we must know the grace and power of being served. For us to lead, we must have a heart that's whole, not broken and empty. For us to be right with those we lead, we must first be right within our own hearts. It's the bedrock of my faith. It's the anchor of my life.

This book is built on the foundation of my leadership core values, which spell **"H.E.A.R.T."**

→ **Humility**
→ **Engagement**
→ **Attitude**
→ **Results**
→ **Today!**

Leadership is a call and charge we choose to answer, and it starts within our very own hearts. It's a matter of our character, behaviors, and the results we create and drive forward. Day in and day out, we are called to love, serve, and lead others. We are challenged to lead people from a current state to a future state.

When you boil it down to its purest form, I believe leaders are called to do 3 things:

1. Champion core values.
2. Develop people (including themselves).
3. Drive greater RESULTS!

Throughout this book, I'll be sharing proven leadership frameworks, strategies, and tools that focus on helping leaders achieve all 3 of these essential aspects of leadership. These truths and principles are only powerful when they're fully implemented in our life and leadership. Through many great teachers and mentors in my life and through the seasons and fires of leadership, I've seen them work to impact and influence people. They've transformed me into the leader I am today.

Let me share a few legacy leaders who have poured these principles into my life and leadership through the years:

- My Dad, teaching me the power of hard work, always pulling up my bootstraps to get the job done.

- My Papa, an Executive Leader with Exxon for over 40 years, taught me to always take pride in the quality of my work.

- Chuck Gartman, my youth minister and mentor, taught me to always "keep on keeping on!"

- Dr. Ken Hall, former President of Buckner International and friend, taught me the importance of passionately caring for your people and mission.

- Barry Blanton, founder of Blanton Advisors and friend, for living the example of always showing up to serve and give to others.

- Mike Ferrell, my high school baseball coach, for always driving me to excellence, nothing less.

- Frankie Alexander, friend and former Executive Director of Leadership Montgomery County, taught me firsthand the power of believing in someone's potential.

- Merlyn Koch, my father-in-law, thank you for your example of faith through life's challenges, teaching me to always "tie another knot"!

- Bob Keonig, a former coach and mentor, taught me the invaluable gift of receiving feedback.

My list could go on and on. As you reflect on those legacy leaders in your life, consider the impact of your life and leadership on those you love, serve, and lead today. What will your legacy be 10, 20, 30 years from now? Legacy is the end game, the sum of our leadership. I hope during our learning journey together, you catch a glimpse of the opportunity and responsibility each day gives us to be legacy leaders.

Maybe you're wondering who this book is for. If you're a new leader, it's for you. You'll find new truths and principles to implement in your leadership immediately. These fundamentals of leadership will **EQUIP YOU.**

If you're a mid-level leader, having led people and teams for a few years, you'll be reminded of leadership truths you already know and hopefully practice. You'll be challenged to consider new mindsets and behaviors. Sometimes we get comfortable, or even stuck, in our ways and need a fresh start and perspective. These fundamentals of leadership will **EMPOWER YOU.**

If you're a seasoned senior leader, you should be teaching this book instead of me! As a seasoned leader like you, I'm grateful for the many years of leadership lessons and experiences. And yet, most days, I feel like I'm just getting started! Remember, friends, there's no finish line to growth.

As a seasoned leader, you will be reminded of the power of legacy. It's our opportunity to pour into others, developing leaders around us. These leadership fundamentals will **ENCOURAGE YOU**.

Some of you, regardless of where you are on your leadership journey, are fighting just to take another step. The weight and burden of leadership gets heavy and sometimes overwhelming. If you're a discouraged leader, this book is for you too. I've been there. It's like living in a skeleton of dry bones. But take heart. I'm here to give you hope and encouragement to keep going. The leadership H.E.A.R.T. principles and truths can cause your heart to start beating again. Stay with me, you'll feel the pounding in your chest soon. Your leadership still matters.

If any of you complete this book and find little or no value from this learning journey together, then I've completely failed. But if only one reader catches a spark of hope or joy in their leadership, then it's been worth it. I dare you to keep reading. You're on the edge of a renewed passion and pursuit of excellence in your life and leadership that will impact YOU and everyone you love, serve, and lead.

Now, let's open the curtain a little further. Let's get real and lean in together. Get eye-to-eye with me for a moment. It's hard for me to put the hope and compelling charge of this book to you in writing, but here's my best attempt:

I DARE YOU to open your heart and mind to new ideas and perspectives.

I DARE YOU to celebrate and own your strengths with a mindset to always grow!

I DARE YOU to establish and align your leadership character, behavior, and results!

I DARE YOU to develop the leaders around you, becoming a legacy leader!

I DARE YOU to unleash **YOUR** heart, igniting a revolution of influence and impact!

Let's Go!

CHAPTER 1

"Heart"

Does leadership really begin in the heart? Our heart is the innermost part of us. It's the vital essence of our life. It's the command center of our soul. It's the wellspring of our lives. It's the source of unspeakable purpose and passion, given to us to be poured out on planet Earth, making life better for those we love, serve, and lead. It's contained in our heart, like a dam, holding deep waters in its boundaries. Was our heart created to hold in or pour out? I believe its purpose is to be poured out. Unleash the powerful flow of love, service, and leadership, impacting hearts for generations to come.

The living waters of our heart are deep, given to us to share with others. People are thirsty for leaders who allow their hearts to freely pour out life-giving character, actions, and hope. Listen carefully. As powerful as these flowing waters can be, we can only unleash the depth of waters we have experienced and know. We can't pour from an empty heart. We can't give to others what we don't know and have ourselves. This truth compels us to strengthen and safeguard our hearts!

Be intentional in aligning your heart with your creator so you can share deep living waters with those you love, lead, and serve. Don't allow dirty, unclean water into your heart. Say no to anything contrary to your heart's core values. Say no to anyone that is not aligned with your heart's values. Say no to habits and activities that cause you to empty your heart instead of filling your heart. Say no to thoughts that talk you down and not up. Read great books. Watch wholesome programs, not those opposite of your values. For your physical heart, be intentional about what you eat and drink. Commit to activities that strengthen your heart, body, mind, and spirit.

Here's a strategy to help you strengthen and safeguard your heart. It's simple but complex. It's called the 3Rs Coaching Technique. First, commit to **RELEASING** bad habits, bad thoughts, and bad relationships that drag you back into the toxic waters. Secondly, commit to **REACHING** new relationships, mindsets, and habits that draw you to deeper waters of life, hope, and impact. These build you up and don't tear you down. Third, commit to **REMAINING** in these new waters of growth, high performance, and greater influence as a leader in all areas of your life.

I promise as you commit to this Release, Reach, and Remain strategy, you will see continuous growth and more abundant joy and results in your life. Learn this strategy. Live this strategy. Lead others with this strategy. This is how to change the world, starting in our own home, workplace, and community.

Our heart reflects our character. Our heart and character live and breathe as one. Every day, with our words and actions, our character collides with those we love, serve, and lead. In the boardroom, in the drive-thru, in the car driving our kids to school, or in a team meeting, our actions reflect the state of our heart. The hope of this book is to help leaders at every level, in every season of life, to better align their character, actions, and results. Consistency is the key. The foundation of our character sits upon our core values, which are a reflection of our heart.

Most leaders and organizations today are dialed into the importance of building strong cultures. I believe culture also counts in our homes, our marriages, our churches, our not-for-profits, and any other gathering of people working together for a mission and cause. Our values align us, starting within our own hearts and collectively with every heart involved. Culture lives or dies upon the consistent practice and accountability of our core values. And leader, it starts with us.

We must clearly define our own core values and then, without hesitation and unapologetically, live them out daily. The H.E.A.R.T. of this book reflects my own core leadership values, applied to every leadership role I play in my life… husband, father, grandfather, son, CEO, community leader, volunteer, etc. Every day, in every situation, I recall these values and do my very best to live them out for others to see. *Humility, engagement, attitude, results, today!* I strive daily to close the gap between my words and my actions.

Humility is the first value we will explore within a leader and hungers and thirsts for feedback. I welcome feedback from my family, spouse, team, and audience to communicate with me when I'm on the mark or especially when I'm off the mark. It's the bedrock of my character muscle. It's how I grow and get better. It's how I maximize my strengths and how I recognize and become intentional in strengthening my weaknesses. It eliminates any blind spots I might have as a leader, husband, parent, or friend.

A recent example of feedback changing my "heart" involved our daughter Jessie becoming my strength and fitness coach. We were vacationing with her recently in Myrtle Beach, South Carolina, and she very lovingly shared her concerns about my gaining weight since I'd last seen her. If you're wondering, it was a slow process of gaining 50 pounds since my playing days at Baylor. It's the most I've ever weighed in my life. Because she cared enough to challenge me with truthful feedback, I've since lost 50 pounds and have become a competitive masters powerlifter. The commitment to change and become healthier with my physical heart has transformed my heart in every other dimension too. I'm full of energy and have a renewed mindset to grow and get better every day. I had the choice to ignore the feedback and stay on the same path of destruction or to receive the feedback, choosing to change and get better. Feedback is a gift to receive and share.

This lesson in feedback and choosing to receive it reminds me of a behavioral theory called the "Locus of Control." I call it the "Law of the Hoola Hoop." Before we go further, visualize a hoola hoop on the ground. And you're standing close to it. We choose every day to have an internal locus of control or external locus of control. People who choose the internal locus, standing in the center of their hoola hoop, take full ownership and accountability of their attitude, behaviors, choices, and results of their life. People who choose an external locus of control do the opposite and stand outside of their hoola hoop. They give complete ownership and accountability of their lives to everyone and anyone but themselves. Oftentimes this is called the "victims' mindset." Even when life is hard, and we all know it can be at times, it's ultimately on us to take charge of our attitudes, actions, and results. I'm reminded, too, as a person of faith, that I have free will. Regardless of the circumstances, I control my life, and I answer for the consequences. I choose whether I'm standing inside or outside the hoola hoop.

The Locus of Control theory reinforces the truth that our heart is the one constant in all of our relationships and circumstances. It's the only heart on planet Earth we can control. In all dimensions of our life, we must commit to safeguarding our hearts physically, mentally, emotionally, relationally, and spiritually. We must keep our heart "hydrated and nourished" so it can function at peak performance.

Our heart represents so much of our life. Just like our physical heart, our leadership heart beats daily and impacts all those around us. What's in our heart shows up in our words and actions. It's our responsibility to make sure we keep our heart clean and healthy.

How do we safeguard our hearts? Here are a few suggestions I've found very helpful.

→ Establish great daily habits. Release anything or anyone that holds us back or tears us down.

→ Learn to align your yes and no to your core values and priorities.

→ Stay focused on your mission.

→ Form an inner circle of friends who love you enough to always tell you the truth in affirmation of correction.

Each of these strategies reflects a promise of taking care of yourself in every dimension. The challenge is to commit to renewing your heart daily so you can consistently live and lead at your best.

From my H.E.A.R.T to yours, I wholeheartedly believe there is something inside each of us telling us there is more to this life than the average or status quo. In his book *If You Want to Walk on Water, You've Got to Get Out of the Boat,* John Ortberg writes, "If you don't get out of the boat, there's a guaranteed certainty that you will never walk on the water. This is an immutable law of nature. *If you want to walk on the water, you've got to get out of the boat.*" There's something inside you calling you to the deep waters, even to walk across them if necessary. To leave the comfort of the boat, representing our comfort zones and routine existence, we have to abandon ourselves to the high calling of God in our lives. Can you hear the call to "rise up dry bones"? Are you ready to set your leadership H.E.A.R.T. free for your life and leadership? Join me and countless others who will answer the call to "unleash their leadership H.E.A.R.T" for greater influence and impact! Let's get out of the boat and dive into the deep waters of our leadership H.E.A.R.T. together.

End of Chapter Questions- HEART: (Read Proverbs 4:23)

1. What resonates with you about your leadership "heart"?

2. Take time to identify anything related to your character you can apply the "Release, Reach, Remain" 3Rs strategy. Share it with an accountability partner. Track your progress and get ready for results!

3. How do you "safeguard" your heart now?

4. Reflect on the analogy of the boat and walking on water. Are you comfortable just sitting in your current "boat" of life and leadership? Do you have the desire for greater joy and fulfillment in your life and leadership? What's keeping you from diving into the deep waters today?

CHAPTER 2

Humility

Humility is the cornerstone of character. Character development is the same thing as leadership development. Character sits upon the foundation of your core values as a leader. It's the bedrock we align our lives and leadership upon. When we align our character, actions, and behaviors upon our foundation of core values, incredible things happen for all those we love, serve, and lead.

Consider the many different leaders you've experienced in your life. Some are good, and others are not so good. I've learned as much from leaders I DON'T WANT TO BE LIKE as I have from those I admire. I've been blessed by numerous leaders who have taught me incredible lessons of effective servant leadership. For that, I'm forever grateful. Not only grateful but inspired to reach greater levels of impact and influence on those I lead. My family, my wife, my team, my church, my community. Remember, it's part of our leadership legacy.

Let's consider two very fundamentally different types of leaders. Or better yet, let's consider a leader versus a "boss." Consider how they compare and contrast.

Leader:	Boss:
Humble	Arrogant
Others centered	Self-centered
Influencer	Controlling
Empowering	Stifling
Inspirational	Threatening
People focused	Task focused
"We" focused	"Me" focused
Servant's heart	Dictatorship
Relational	Transactional
Builds trust	Intimidates, builds fear
Responds	Reacts
Adds value	Subtracts value
Effective	Destructive
Willing followers	Forced laborers
Listens	Barks orders

The comparison and contrast could go on and on. I believe it boils down to a single question: Do you follow a leader or a boss, aka "boss-hole"? Yes, there's a distinct picture created by both words. I hope the phrase "boss-hole" creates a strong reaction within you. Not to offend you but to spark a serious introspection of your leadership heart and posture. There's too much at stake within our homes, workplaces, communities, and world to allow bad leadership or "boss-holes" to be in charge.

I believe leaders are "hope givers" to their people. Leadership is an incredible responsibility and opportunity to love, serve, and lead others. Leadership directly impacts the trajectory of people, families, marriages, and organizations. A humble leader recognizes this responsibility and stewards with an intentional effort to make things better because they were there. Legacy leaders make things better than it was before they arrived. Call it the fruits of their labor or simply creating better results. Their leadership mattered.

Humble leaders with a solid foundation of character and core values focus on the legitimate physical, emotional, and spiritual needs of their people. Let's look at specific expressions of humility within a leader.

Humble leaders....

→ Have a strong sense of self-worth, recognize their own strengths and weaknesses, and are committed to growth and continuous improvement.

→ Have this same belief about people, showing high regard for the unique value each person adds.

→ Have great respect for the dignity of all people.

→ Have a great appreciation for their people.

→ Listen to others, giving voice to others.

→ Give and ask for open communication.

→ Demonstrate honesty in all situations.

→ Show affection and compassion (appropriately).

→ Have a consistent pattern (character, attitude, behavior).

→ Build others up, encouraging them from the balcony.

→ Establish healthy boundaries.

→ Establish and reinforce clear and high expectations!

→ Provide consistent accountability for self and others

→ Delivers feedback to affirm and correct, always focused on developing others

→ Invite and embrace feedback!

When a leader is humble, serving and sacrificing for their people, and identifying and meeting needs, they will reap great levels of influence and develop stronger followers. You've heard the myths about humility and humble leaders as being "wimps," "doormats," and frankly weak people. Some have even said it's like giving the asylum over to the inmates, oftentimes turning the organization upside down. From my experience and perspective, this is a total misunderstanding of what a humble leader represents. For me, humility is the strongest posture on planet Earth any leader could strive to become.

Let me share some examples of humble leaders and their actions that convince me to pursue the posture of humility at all costs:

1. Jesus lived, led, taught, and died for his followers. He established clear expectations and values, lived them out, and died to protect and save his people. His teachings and life examples have been multiplied around the world. The principles and truths He taught have changed my life and countless others. His impact is still alive and making a difference today.

2. Humble leaders know how to "spank you" and give you a "hug" at the same time. Think about it. We oftentimes need encouragement and praise, but also tons of correction. They can do both, maintaining your dignity while reinforcing the value and expectation when we fall short on. My Dad was the master of this in my life!

3. Humble leaders can build relationships and still complete the most important tasks at hand.

4. Humble leaders expect excellence, not mediocrity because they believe in the high value and potential within themselves and others.

5. Humble leaders are unapologetic and relentless in sharing and protecting their core values.

6. Humble leaders speak the truth in love, both affirmation and correction.

7. Humble leaders are masters at giving and receiving feedback.

8. Humble leaders reflect attributes of love, kindness, gentleness, patience, goodness, faithfulness, joy, peace, and self-control.

So, now that we've spent some time comparing and contrasting a humble leader with an arrogant "boss-hole," can you imagine following a leader that's not aligned with humility? Would you want your people to experience anything less?

So, how do we improve our posture of humility? There are several ways I use within my own life and for those I coach. Let me share them with you now.

1. *Establish a coaching relationship that focuses on giving you rigorous feedback, challenge, and support.* Coaching can help identify any blind spots. In my coaching relationships, I utilize a 360 Feedback tool to help measure a leader's character, behavior, and results. For the humility and character piece, it simply asks these types of questions, answered by you, the leader, and by those you lead:

→ Do you demonstrate patience and self-control with others?

→ Do you show appreciation and kindness to others?

→ Do you show respect for all people?

→ Do you forgive others for their mistakes?

→ Do you demonstrate humility or arrogance?

→ Are you consistently trustworthy?

→ Do you keep your word?

→ Are you resilient?

→ Do you build others up or tear them down?

Once you've rated yourself and your team submits their ratings of what it's like under your leadership authority, we create a comparison between self-rating and peer-rating. The power of this process can reinforce strengths while shining light on areas for improvement. It will identify blind spots between your self-perception and the perception of your team. It will identify overconfidence and underconfidence within a leader. Having the courage and humility to invite and receive this feedback sets excellent and mediocre leaders apart! It's the difference between being humble and arrogant. Embracing feedback is a nonnegotiable to becoming a humble leader.

2. *Invest in your own growth through educational resources and learning experiences.* is another great development tool. My personal growth plan involves spending time reading great books, meeting with great leaders over coffee or a meal, and keeping a journal to reflect and process the new learnings. Attending roundtables, conferences, podcasts, etc., can all add fresh water to our mind and heart.

3. *Learn from life's challenges and failures.* We have the opportunity to stay humble and grow or remain arrogant and stagnant. We can own our mistakes and circumstances, or we can push the blame and responsibility on everyone else but our own heart. Remember the Law of the Hoola Hoop? Focusing on taking full ownership of our attitude, actions, regardless of what life is throwing our way, allows us to be accountable for our results. This produces growth and maturity in our lives. A growing and mature leader paints a great picture of humility for others to see.

Remember, our heart and character collide with people every day through our attitude and behavior. Our leadership actions are a direct reflection of what's inside of our heart. Relentlessly pursuing a humble heart takes intentional focus, commitment, and resolve. It also takes grace and forgiveness for us and for others. Perform the "mirror" test every day. Make sure the person in the mirror (YOU!) is right on the inside, so you can be right on the outside.

In closing this chapter, remember that the spirit within humble leaders believes, "I've not arrived yet, and I'm not where I hope to be someday, but I'm closer than I was yesterday!" The goal is progress, not perfection. Stay real with your people. Show transparency. Fail forward by admitting your mistakes and sharing what you learn in the process. Love and demonstrate compassion. People are hungry for humble leaders who live these traits out every day. It inspires others to grow and follow your lead. Humble leaders invite others to join them on the journey. Arrogant leaders are often on a lonely walk by themselves. So, which way does the leadership posture "needle" point in your life? Humility or Arrogance? Leader or "boss-hole"? Always remember, the choice is yours.

End of Chapter Questions- Humility (Read Colossians 3:12-16)

1. What resonates most with you from the comparison of humility versus arrogance? Leader vs. a "boss-hole"?

2. What can you release in your posture that moves you closer to humility than arrogance? What new attitudes, beliefs, or habits can you begin building to help you become humbler?

3. How can you integrate feedback into your own leadership growth? Your team?

4. What are the critical next steps for you to take in becoming a more humble leader?

5. Take time this week to write a letter of gratitude to a humble leader who has impacted your life and leadership. Tell them how they've influenced you. They'll be forever blessed, and you will be too!

CHAPTER 3

Engage

The very first automobile I learned to drive was a 1980 Volkswagen Beetle. "Four on the floor," I remember my dad saying. There was a long stick with a knob coming out of the floor. It was between the passenger seat and driver's seat. Some of you may be asking, "A stick?" It was a gear shift stick. Yes, we actually changed the gears manually to drive forward down the road. I went through a few clutches in the process, and I can still remember the sound of the grind when the motor wasn't quite in gear. You're laughing with me now, right? You remember!

The example of shifting gears reminds me of the power of engagement, the next core value we will discuss. When we have our lives "in gear," we can create incredible speed forward. When our life is not "in gear," it's often a miserable grind with multiple costs, not to mention a lack of any forward movement.

The power of being fully engaged in all dimensions of our lives is where we begin to experience life to its fullest. As leaders, we all want to perform at our very best and with a high level of performance for our people and team. We want the very same for the people we love, serve, and lead. Creating the mindset and habits to maximize our performance is what this chapter is all about. So, push in the clutch, and put your leadership in gear. Let's Go!

Full engagement is not about going full speed, racing through life in every direction, forgetting to pause and consider who we want to be and where we truly want to be headed. It seems like the first 30 seconds of every conversation I have with people, it includes the phrase, "I'm so busy." Many of the clients I'm coaching struggle with the reality of balancing the busyness in their lives with their workplace demands. When I visit with couples, there's usually some aspect of "we're just so busy." We are all busy. Busy and productive are two very different things. If you only remember one truth from this chapter on engagement, I encourage you to consider the invaluable resource of your energy. Not your time. Not the tech devices that guide you through the day. Not your credentials, but your energy.

Consider the following scenarios:

- You set aside a "date night" with your spouse and make a big deal about how important it will be for the two of you to spend some "quality time" together. You plan a special meal at a special place. You dress up for the occasion. By the time the appetizer arrives, you've been distracted by your to-do list at work the next day, continue to feel the vibration of messages going off from your phone, and you've lost the special moment because you're not "fully" present.

- You make appointments on your calendar, strive all day to meet and complete every meeting, but you've not made time for yourself to rest, reflect, and process anything that's happened during the day, and your energy turns into irritation, lack of motivation, and a desire to simply leave the office.

- You have a team meeting in an hour, but you've allowed every text and email dinging on your phone to distract you from preparing your mind for the presentation. Your hope for a powerful message turns into a rote exercise of boring information.

So, all of this to say, our maximum performance in every dimension of our lives is grounded in the intentional management of our energy. As leaders, we are stewards of organizational energy too. We must learn it, live it, and lead it for it to truly transform our people and organization.

To be "fully engaged," we must be:

→ physically strong and energized

→ emotionally stable and connected

→ mentally aware and focused

→ spiritually aligned with our purpose, passion, and core values

Regardless of our circumstances or immediate situation, we must pursue full engagement in every dimension of our lives. This mindset and lifestyle can be a significant shift in how you live your life. Research tells us that a majority of people are not "fully engaged" in their lives at home, work, or community. We see it everywhere.

When I consult with prospective nonprofit leaders, one of the first priorities they present to me is how to "engage" their board of directors. Leaders struggle with engaging their teams. Struggling and frustrated spouses often say their partner is checked out and "not engaged" in the marriage. It's truly one of the costliest realities today in corporate America, nonprofits, and in our homes.

Let's consider two very different paradigms of "Full Engagement":

Old Paradigm:	**New Paradigm:**
Time management	Energy Management
Stress management and avoidance	Healthy tension and stress
Life is a marathon	Life is a series of intervals
Downtime is lazy and wasteful	Downtime is refreshing and productive
Self-discipline rules	Rituals and habits rule
Positive thinking solves it	Power of full engagement solves it
Fully committed	Fully present

Which column reflects your mindset and understanding of "full engagement"? Let's consider implementing the new paradigm mindset in our life and leadership.

One of my favorite metaphors for learning life lessons is through athletics. I grew up with a dad who was a collegiate football star and head football coach for much of my childhood. I was blessed to play baseball from the time I was seven years old until finishing my career at Baylor University, taking my last swing at the Southwest Conference Championship in Fayetteville, Arkansas. Our family lived and breathed athletics.

Let this fact sink in—competitive athletes spend approximately 90% of their time training in order to perform and compete 10% of the time. They build routines that last year-round. Their entire lives are designed to sustain and renew energy for specific periods of time. They build in times of intense training for rigorous competition and intentional times for healing, rest, and renewal. For most of us, our "off-season" break is a day off here and there, or maybe a long weekend, and if we're really fortunate, a two-week vacation once a year. These times away from work usually involve work emails, text messages, and phone calls, if we're honest. So here's a question: If athletes can create a rhythm of 90/10 training to performance and periods of rest and recovery, why can't we, as ordinary leaders, master this rhythm? How can we create the same 90/10 rule in our lives and leadership without sacrificing our health, happiness, and passion for life? Yep, you know the answer. We must learn to become "fully engaged," drawing on energy from our physical, emotional, mental, and spiritual dimensions of ourselves.

The goal of "full engagement" is to find a way to not overuse or underuse our energy in any dimension. To find and live a consistent pattern of expending energy and renewing our energy. Think about the physical markers of energy capacity. They consist of our strength, endurance, flexibility, and resilience. These are exactly the same markers in all other dimensions of our lives. Consider stretching and flexibility. It's one thing to stretch your hamstrings, but how well do we have the ability to flex our emotional muscles along a wide spectrum of experiences? Can we move freely and appropriately along a wide assortment of emotions? Do we have the emotional resilience to withstand and bounce back from really tough circumstances, disappointments, or even loss? What about your mental focus? Can you withstand a marathon of tasks and demands and remain focused and attentive? How about your spiritual muscles? Are you able to stand up and risk everything for the values and people you love, even if it requires great personal sacrifice? As you can see, to be "fully engaged" requires incredible strength, resolve, flexibility, and resilience in all dimensions of our lives.

Let's discuss a few strategies on how to strengthen our capacity to be "fully engaged" in all dimensions. One of my favorites is John Maxwell's "Law of the Rubber Band." When you think about a rubber band, what was it designed and intended to do? Yes, to hold things together, which requires the rubber band to stretch to some degree without breaking! As mentioned in the new paradigm of full engagement, stress is not a bad thing in our lives if it's given the opportunity to stretch and push us beyond our comfort zone and normal limits. Like athletes, this process builds strength by tearing down the muscle fibers, and by the end of the training session, fatigue and functional capacity are diminished. But with rest and recovery, the muscles not only repair but oftentimes come back even stronger. We build emotional, mental, and spiritual capacity the very same way we do physically.

As you know, full engagement often starts within our hearts and minds. To make sure there is nothing blocking you from desiring or achieving greater engagement in all areas of your life, I want to remind you about a simple yet powerful mindset tool I use with all my coaching clients. I've shared it with you earlier in the book. It's the "3R" technique. Release, Reach, Remain. Here's how it applies to "full engagement." First, identify habits, mindsets, and people who are holding you back or talking you down. In other words, anything toxic or negative that hinders you from being your very best in every dimension. Name these things specifically.

Sometimes, I have a client actually face a wall and put these on sticky notes so they can see them. Next, turn away from the wall and face a new wall opposite from where your "release" wall is. You've just "repented" and turned 180 degrees from these things.

Now, name new habits, mindsets, people, and goals you wish to achieve in your life and leadership. These become your new targets and hopes you are reaching toward. Name them specifically. Build specific action steps for each one. Commit to pursuing these daily. Stay focused and determined.

Lastly, after you've achieved your new wall of hopes and targets, commit to remaining in them! Make these nonnegotiables in your life. No more going back, but only forward to new growth. It's the promise of implementing the 3Rs... release, reach, and remain. To maximize your full engagement, the process must continue for the rest of your life. Why? Because there is no finish line to your growth!

The discipline of "daily grind" will compound positive results in your life and leadership. Commit to this mindset in every dimension of your life.

Physically: Commit daily to good nutrition, working out, stretching, and strengthening your heart, mind, body, and soul. For me, working out and pursuing competitive powerlifting goals fills my tank in every dimension of my life. It's purposeful and intentional. It's a priority. Time and resources are invested. This discipline will impact your attitude, performance, and strength in all dimensions.

Mentally: Be sure to read and listen to good books and spend time meditating and reflecting. These disciplines restore our mind and spirit.

Emotionally: Focus on establishing healthy boundaries. Invest in rich relationships, building an inner circle of friends to share and listen to one another.

Spiritually: Intentionally practice the disciplines of prayer, worship, Bible study, discipleship, giving, serving, and growing.

All of these disciplines and habits actually reflect core values for self-care, personal growth, maximum performance, and helping others. The daily grind of these habits and disciplines is the bedrock for our growth and full engagement. It's a lifelong road of obedience to these disciplines that delivers abundant joy and living fully engaged lives.

Establish a rhythm of exertion, rest, recovery, reflection, recharge, and REPEAT! Remember, we can't give what we don't know and have, and an empty cup is worthless in helping ourselves and others. For my powerlifting workouts, my coach and daughter Jessie creates 12-week programs for me to follow. It's very much like the 90-day mindset for setting goals and tracking progress I use in my leadership coaching. The 12-week program cycles me through times of intense lifting, peak meet performance preparations, deloads after a meet or intense cycle, and periods of rest. It's built on the model athletes teach us. It works. Remember to give yourself the freedom and grace to adjust or abandon your current schedule to deal with the promised challenges of life.

Full engagement is a lifelong lifestyle. We all have seasons in life where we need to pivot and adjust. During these times, remember the things you can control. Give those things your best energy. If we fall, we get back up. If we fail, we learn and keep going forward.

As a leadership coach, I remind leaders and organizations to invest in times of growth, reflection, and restful recharge for their people. Every leader needs it to thrive. In our marriage, Liz and I commit every January or February to go away for the week. Our purpose is to enjoy undivided time and attention with one another. We also spend intentional time reflecting on the past year, discussing any changes we need to make in our marriage, finances, and family moving forward. We name the changes and commit to two or three priorities for the coming year. We've done this now for 16 of our 16 years of marriage. It's a nonnegotiable for our marriage. It's a highlight for us. I hope more companies and marriages commit to times of rest, reflection, restoration, and recharge.

I use a tool called the "wheel of life" to show people where they are experiencing full engagement in areas of their lives and also places that need immediate improvement and adjustment. I've included one of these for you in the resource section at the end book. This tool creates specific growth targets for you to increase your engagement in very specific areas, therefore giving you a fully inflated "tire" to live on!

My hope is you're totally sold out to the new paradigm of full engagement in your life and leadership. Imagine how much more fun, productive, and fulfilling your life will be in every dimension! This process is the foundation of maximizing your God-given potential and unique talents to make life better for those you love, serve, and lead. Just think. What if you were fully engaged in your marriage, family, and team? The impact and implications are limitless. So, stop grinding gears, and get in gear. Unleash the power and potential of your heart in every dimension. The world will be a better place because of it.

End of Chapter Questions- Engagement (Read Philippians 3:12-14)

1. What resonates most with you about the concept of "full engagement"?

2. What "old paradigm" of full engagement characteristics will be the most challenging to release for you? What is most inspiring about the "new paradigm" of full engagement?

3. Which dimension do you feel you are fully engaged in? Which dimension needs the most transformation in your life to become more fully engaged?

4. What are the critical next steps for you to take in becoming a more "fully engaged" leader?

5. Complete the "wheel of life" exercise. Identify 1 dimension on the wheel you will commit to be more intentional in becoming more "inflated" and engaged. Identify 2-3 action steps that will move you in that direction. Track it. Journal it. Ask a friend to be an accountability partner for you in this journey. Once you develop this dimension, repeat the same steps for your next area of growth. Repeat this cycle from now on and watch your results soar!

CHAPTER 4

Attitude

Our attitude enters the room before we even say a word. You've felt it before, right? A person approaches you, and you can read their attitude. You can feel their attitude. It's often the most powerful message you receive from the person. Like our body language, attitude can shout louder than any word or message we ever try to deliver. Attitude is mindset. It's reflected from a deep core posture within our heart. Like our heart, our attitude is a clear reflection of what's on the inside.

Here are some of my favorite attitude quotes. I dare you to read them again. Consider how they impact you.

→ *"We cannot change our past. We cannot change the fact that people act in a certain way. We cannot change the inevitable. The only thing we can do is play on the one string we have, and that is our attitude."* - Chuck Swindoll

→ *"People may hear your words, but they feel your attitude"* - John Maxwell

→ *"You can't control what happens to you, but you can control your attitude toward what happens to you, and in that, you will be mastering change rather than allowing it to master you"* - Brian Tracy

➔ *"Weakness of attitude becomes weakness of character"* - Albert Einstein

➔ *"Everything can be taken from a man but one thing: the last of human freedoms... to choose one's attitude in any given set of circumstances, to choose one's own way."* - Victor Frankl

Let me share a few of the "attitude" mindsets I've been taught through the years and continue to follow:

1. ***"Double dog dare!"*** How many of you get fired up when you hear the phrase "I dare you!" Like the famous line in the movie *A Christmas Story*, this phrase creates a strong desire to leave the status quo and boring things behind, immediately searching for the next challenge! This attitude reflects the truth of John Maxwell's "Law of the Lid," reminding us that we each are given an incredible gifting of talents to be maximized on planet Earth for the betterment of all! This attitude leaves the lazy behind and even makes them weary thinking about it. It calls for the courage to be swift and daring. Don't settle for less, go for your best. The "lid" we allow to limit our growth or become our ceiling directly impacts our joy and performance in life. When we look for intentional ways to grow and get better, we raise our "lid." If I'm currently performing at a 7, this attitude asks, "How can I become an 8?" If I'm performing at a 10, "How can I get to 11?" There's no finish line to growth and progress within this "I dare you" attitude mindset. Join me, and let's increase the number of the "priceless few" who embrace and live out this attitude in all areas of their lives. Friends, this attitude is contagious. Unleash this attitude in all dimensions of your life and watch your results soar!

2. ***"Keep on keeping on!"*** Persistence (aka "stubbornness!") drives us forward regardless of what's ahead. Chuck Gartman, who I've mentioned earlier, always ended his correspondence with the phrase,

"Keep on keeping on." I've been using "keep on" or "lead on" ever since. It's the "Little Engine that Could"...I think I can, etc. It's my Father-in-Law Meryln reminding me to "tie another knot" when things get tough. It's my Dad Charlie reminding me to "pull up my bootstraps" when I think I can't go another step. It's the pursuit of completion, not quitting.

3. *"The Law of the Hoola Hoop"* principles of ownership, accountability, and results I've mentioned earlier in the book is about mindset. Being the responsible adult that takes full ownership and accountability for their lives, regardless of the circumstances, knowing without a doubt they shape and drive the results in their own lives.

4. *"The opposite of love is indifference."* Love is action. This phrase convicts me to love people deeply. To stay engaged. To stay present. To walk beside people, even our enemies at times. The attitude and action of love in our lives and leadership is something people will never forget.

5. *"Gratitude is attitude."* Staying focused on all we have and not our deficits is so important. Frankly, I'm spoiled rotten. I have more than I'll ever need and certainly deserve. People see right to the heart of our attitudes. We can't hide it, or certainly not fake it. It's important for people to see, hear, and experience gratitude in our actions and responses. Lead by example, showing thanks to those who serve and love you. Look for the one good thing to keep you going. My faith heritage teaches me, over and over, that gratitude is the right attitude.

6. *"Excellence over mediocrity every time!"* As a youth, my mom, who was a concert pianist, and my Papa, who was an executive leader for Exxon for 45 years, reminded me to keep practicing piano and baseball, always trying to be the very best! Good enough is never good

enough, regardless of what you're doing or attempting. Confront every attitude focused on "that's how we've always done it!" This attitude drives me absolutely crazy as a leader.

Side note: if you believe in this thought of "this is how we've always done it," then please stop and reread this chapter on attitude. Leaders, our attitude is extremely contagious. Remind yourself and people to grow and take risks, failing forward, learning from every experience, and always getting back up to try again, and again, and again for better. For me, it's reflected in the heart of a lion. Relentlessly in pursuit of excellence. It causes my heart to *"ROAR!"*

Before I conclude this section, let me expand and get close up and personal with you. Let me open up the "curtain" of my life and examine the raw reality of this attitude together. This attitude is one we read about throughout scripture. Chapter One of James teaches us to *"Consider it pure joy when you face trials, for it builds your character."* The whole joy thing when it's tough, oftentimes, is the absolute last thing I feel. I'm sure you, too, have experienced some of life's most difficult and challenging circumstances. The pain of struggle and loss can be paralyzing. Seeing a tough situation as an opportunity to grow is not always my first thought. But down deep, I believe it. My faith teaches me to embrace painful experiences as a pathway to incredible growth.

Often, our true self shows up when things are hard. Hard times define and reveal our character and certainly our attitude. Recently, I lost my only sister Julie at the young age of 48. She was adopted by my parents when I was 8. I can remember the day my parents came to get me from school to go and pick her up in Houston. My parents went through an adoption agency, and Julie was only three weeks old. I was the very first one to meet her and hold her. Handing her to my parents is a day I still remember. Fast forward 50 years, and now she's gone. Forever. My sister battled many adversities throughout her life, including drug addiction, severe diabetes, and homelessness. I've witnessed my parents experience many painful lessons of "tough love" and incredible grace with Julie. There were times we didn't even know where Julie was for long periods of time. Fortunately, the past few years were somewhat peaceful and really good for Julie and my parents. As a family, we experienced firsthand the power of grace and forgiveness, always seeking to reconcile and make things right. We experienced the pain of disagreement, intense conflict, and periods of high anxiety and worry. Thankfully, in every circumstance and season, our family remained faithful to Julie and one another.

The last few days and hours with Julie were some of the most peaceful and courageous encounters we've had with one another, especially with her. The courage on her face when she heard the words "hospice care" is still chilling to me today. At a time of great pain and potential fear, she remained courageous and calm. She understood and was at peace. Just like being the very first one to see her and welcome her to our family in the beginning, ironically, I was the very last one to tell her I loved her while telling her goodbye one afternoon in the ICU. She was being transported to hospice care, and we were going to visit her there once she arrived by ambulance. She passed away shortly thereafter. I was blessed to officiate her "celebration of life" service. Hundreds of friends came to celebrate my sister and encourage our family. It was a beautiful experience I will never forget.

So, all that to say, one of the greatest truths reinforced throughout this period of time was the value of staying focused on the beauty, not the ashes. Embracing the joy, not dwelling on the pain. Strengthening our love for one another, not becoming bitter and divided. Growth and maturity do come through the trials, challenges, and pains we encounter. Not if we encounter them but when we walk through them. I'm forever grateful for the example of courage and peace Julie showed in the last days, hours, and breaths of her life.

I love you, sister, and thanks for teaching me, your big brother, this life-giving truth about attitude. Remember, the attitude of joy amidst challenges.

Now, let's shift gears and review a list of 8 attitudes given to us two thousand years ago. Many of you remember the "beatitudes" Jesus taught in the Sermon on the Mount. These teachings were the first and longest lessons shared by Jesus. They paint a clear picture of the "attitudes" He seeks for His people. It's fascinating to me how they describe the desirable attitude ("if") with a clear result ("then"). These attitudes are an "if" and "then" proposition. It's also very significant how each beatitude is introduced. It clearly states, "Blessed are those" who live these attitudes. It qualifies these people as truly blessed. It reflects a posture of deep gratitude for the teacher delivering these lessons and commands. The humble servant leader Jesus lived these out, and His people experienced it firsthand. Therefore, they recognized the source of their blessed state, and many chose to follow Him.

Let's see how these can be applied to our leadership:

1. *"Blessed are those who are 'poor in spirit' for The Kingdom of Heaven is yours."*

Beatitude ("if") > Result ("then")

Description: Leaders are humble, "boss-holes" are arrogant. Free in spirit. Delivered from bondage, secure in who they are. Focused on helping others find freedom. Repentant heart, always willing to grow, mature, and transform.

Leadership relevance: As leaders, we must choose the posture of humility, like we've been discussing. The freedom within our hearts to lead with humility breeds humility in others. One of the greatest strengths of a humble leader is the willingness and courage to be vulnerable. The security of being a vulnerable leader creates freedom within the team. People crave real leaders. This beatitude also reminds leaders of the power of a repentant heart, having the ability and desire to change an attitude or behavior for the better. The repentant, humble, and free leader builds a deep level of trust and credibility within the team. Every home, workplace, and community needs humble leaders to courageously champion these values and attitudes.

2. *"Blessed are those who mourn, for they will be comforted."*

Beatitude ("if") > Result ("then")

<u>Description</u>: Deeply concerned for others. Shares hope and shows compassion to others.

<u>Leadership relevance</u>: I don't know about you, but it's probably safe to say there are people on your team, maybe even you, who are hurting deeply. Life is happening at speeds we can't even quantify, and lives are oftentimes stressed and upside down. This beatitude reminds us of the powerful attitude of compassion. I've found the best way to express this attitude is to simply show up for people. Sometimes our presence and concern truly comfort people in their pain and stress. This beatitude is worthless if it's not completely authentic. Love is a powerful word and is action-oriented at its very core. To show compassion for our people, with genuine concern, gives hope and comfort to people beyond the current situation. Don't forget leaders, it's good for us to receive this very same beatitude from our people too.

3. *"Blessed are the meek, for they will inherit the earth."*

Beatitude ("if") > Result (then")

<u>Description</u>: Gentle, self-controlled, free from malice, and having a condescending spirit. Strong sense of security, able to champion the needs of others.

<u>Leadership relevance</u>: Remember the comparison between a humble leader and an arrogant "boss-hole"? This beatitude captures the very essence of the gentle, self-controlled, and secure leader, in contrast to an out-of-control,

harsh boss. We've all experienced both, I'm sure. The gentle, humble leader will create a culture free of malice and toxic talk. This leadership beatitude promises to eliminate negative and condescending words and actions. Meek leaders are strong, always championing the values and needs of their people. This beatitude calls leaders to be proactive, not reactive. Gentle leaders build their people up, not tearing them down with low expectations or demeaning feedback. Remember, meekness and humility are not weak postures indicative of a "doormat" attitude or posture. They are strong in their convictions and commitment to protect, defend, and lead their team with excellence.

4. *"Blessed are those who hunger & thirst for righteousness, for they will be filled."*

Beatitude ("if") > Result (then")

Description: Deeply fulfilled, high levels of passion. Able to lift up and encourage others. Willing to stand for what's right. Consistently confronts social justice.

Leadership relevance: How many leaders or people do you know walking through life with zero fulfillment and zero passion in their life? Is this you? I find someone almost every week in this current state of despair and emptiness. If I'm a leader who hungers and thirsts for righteousness, it means I'm grounded in a deep sense of purpose and passion for my life and leadership. Fulfilled leaders help others find fulfillment. Always fighting fiercely for what's right gives hope and confidence to people. Confronting issues, attitudes, and even people who threaten justice or bring destructive tendencies to the team, or family, is a consistent action leaders take within this beatitude. This leadership attitude reflects integrity in action. This is a leader who consistently lives and leads with deep conviction.

5. *"Blessed are the merciful, for they will be shown mercy."*

Beatitude ("if") > Result (then")

Description: Forgiveness is freely given and received. Shows kindness and is tolerant of others. Intentional focus on seeing and healing wounds. Compassionate and non-judgmental.

Leadership relevance: Mercy is an undeserved gift I've received countless times in my life, and leadership. Do you know what it feels like to receive mercy? Again, we can't give what we don't know or have not received ourselves first. This beatitude convicts me, too, about the gift of forgiveness. Like mercy, if a leader has experienced the gift of forgiveness, they are more likely and capable of forgiving others. And themselves. I believe leaders must take the initiative in giving mercy and forgiveness. One action of mercy can transform a family, team, organization, and community. If you're stuck in this area, please seek counsel and help. The inability or unwillingness to give or receive forgiveness and mercy can be crippling for your life and leadership. I see this in my coaching relationships. When a leader is set free through mercy or forgiveness, it's a game changer for their life and leadership. This beatitude of mercy reminds us all to be kind to one another. Kindness also reflects patience and tolerance. The world needs more of this beatitude. When we show and deliver genuine kindness, mercy, and forgiveness, we can help people through their hurts, wounds, and problems. Lastly, this beatitude calls us to be reconcilers. When things are broken or just not right, leaders directly address it and help make it right.

6. *"Blessed are the pure in heart, for they will see God."*

Beatitude ("if") > Result (then")

Description: Puts love in action. Character influences others to willingly follow.

Leadership relevance: As we've been discussing, our leadership attitude, actions, and behaviors are a direct reflection of our hearts. Our heart collides with those we love, serve, and lead every day. The charge of this beatitude is to keep our hearts pure so we can truly love and lead people well. Centered in pure motives, our actions of love and leadership will cause people to follow. Leaders with pure hearts cause people to grow and achieve greater potential and results in their lives. Remember, we must safeguard and strengthen our hearts every day. We're the only ones who can do that for our own heart. When our heart is right, we can then help others with theirs.

7. *"Blessed are the peacemakers, for they will be called Sons of God."*

Beatitude ("if") > Result (then")

Description: Unity builder. Builds trust and unity within all teams. Solution-focused. Conflict resolution is nonnegotiable.

Leadership relevance: What's the opposite of peace? DRAMA!! Oh my, don't we see drama spreading like wildfire these days in our country and in the workplace. With all of the anxiety, conflict, and unrest we face today, leaders have a great platform to address this through their beatitude of being a peacemaker. Our opportunity is to build unity, not division. To build trust, not distrust. Even families need leaders within the home to do the very same each and every day. Being a peacemaker doesn't mean compromising your values, but it might mean compromising your expectations with others to achieve a goal. Being a peacemaker means we focus on solutions. Being a peacemaker means we step into conflict with the absolute goal to reconcile and resolve differences. It's not **IF** we face conflict, but **WHEN** we face it. Leading with the beatitude of peace can build teamwork and help tear down walls of divide and isolation. It's not an easy task, but one that we must always stay the course without delay or denial. To sum this up for me, it's remembering to commit to unity among diversity in thought, ideas, and solutions without compromising core values.

8. *"Blessed are those persecuted for justice, for theirs is the Kingdom of Heaven."*

Beatitude ("if") > Result (then")

Description: Champions values. Leads by example. Confronts injustice and rights all wrongs.

Leadership relevance: This beatitude challenges me and leaders to remain steadfast in living out core values on a consistent basis. Leaders address injustice head-on, withstanding the opposition and pain it will likely cause. The greatest threat sometimes to a leader and a team is to allow inconsistencies in values, attitudes, and behaviors to exist. In other words, not holding everyone accountable to the same values, policies, expectations, and performance measures can create a sense of injustice within a team. It's terribly destructive and undermines the health of a family, team, and organization. So, lead by example. Eliminate any hypocrisy in your life and leadership. Assess and measure the consistency of your cultural values across all levels of the organization. Ensure a fair process for people to follow when they feel mistreated. Create a culture of feedback and accountability so concerns about inconsistencies and injustices can be addressed fairly, confidentially, and without any hesitation or retaliation.

As we wrap up this chapter on attitude, I encourage you to read through these beatitudes again. And again. If you're like me, I have a long way to grow with my attitude reflecting these "beatitude" characteristics and convictions consistently. I'm aware of and working on them daily. Remember, like our heart, our attitude is a muscle we can change, grow, and strengthen. Start the attitude adjustment process today!

End of Chapter Questions- Attitude (Read Philippians 4:8-9)

1. What positive attitude(s) do people recognize in you? What's your strongest one?

2. Do you see any application of the "beatitudes" for your leadership today? Which one will you begin a growth plan on?

3. What "attitudes" have been impressed upon you in your life and leadership? How do you live them out daily?

4. Life is not always what it's supposed to be. It's the way it is! How do you cope with this reality? What can you do to create a springboard for using tough times and pain to help you grow?

5. Remember, where there is no struggle, there is no real progress. What challenges have you been ignoring or procrastinating dealing with? What can you do to address it head-on this next week?

CHAPTER 5

Results

We are the consequences of our choices and behavior. We reap what we sow. Good or bad, consequences are brought to life in our lives through our actions. It's one of the oldest truths still applicable today.

Before we go any further, let me clarify a fundamental belief and truth I believe about consequences, good or bad. Yes, we directly cause consequences in our lives daily through our decisions and actions. And, sometimes, there are consequences that collide with us that have nothing to do with us at all. It's called life. Some very good, some very difficult, and just plain bad. As we discussed in the previous chapter, it's ultimately our choice as to how we respond to life's challenges and victories as a result of our own choices or simply a consequence of living on planet Earth.

It's the "Law of the Hoola Hoop" again. We either take full ownership, responsibility, and accountability for our consequences, or we push all of these on everyone but ourselves. Internal locus of control versus external locus of control. I like to sum this principle and law up as the "Law of the OAR." Ownership. Accountability Results. It's a daily choice in every leadership role we step into.

Let me also say with deep conviction that even as a person of faith, I ultimately have "free will" to make choices hourly. Even in the most difficult of circumstances, we have the ability to choose our response. Some days we get it, and some days, we fall short, but as a responsible leader, and adult, I accept the responsibility 100%.

It would be fun to hear your list of who you consider the most successful people on earth. Who would be your choice for "GOAT" (greatest of all time) in sports, music, entertainment, business, ministry, parenting, and leadership? What about their life, talents, reputation, and performance caused you to put them on your list? Odds are it is directly related to the positive consequences or RESULTS they created in and through their lives. Results are defined as a result of or consequence of an action. I believe we were created and designed to cause results in our lives and in the lives of those we love, serve, and lead.

Let me share some guiding principles about RESULTS that have inspired me and will hopefully give you encouragement and possibly new ways of living out your life and leadership each day. Stewardship is the first principle that compels a drive for greater results in my life and leadership. It's a biblical principle I've been trying to master my entire adult life. We are responsible and accountable for the gifts, talents, people, opportunities, and resources we've been entrusted to make life better for those we love, serve, and lead. In my life and leadership, I hope to hear, "Well done my good and faithful servant." In my organization, I hope to hear people say it's better now than it was before I started serving and leading. As a nonprofit executive leader, I hope the "bottom line" of our organization, which is focused on "lives impacted," along with our financial sustainability, is strengthened under my leadership. For donors, my hope is to increase tangible ROI (return on investment). In my marriage, I hope my wife and family see fruits of growth, joy, and an unwavering commitment, encouraging every couple we meet in our pursuit of excellence and getting better. So, what areas of your life and leadership do you consider the responsibility of stewardship? I'll give you a chance to respond to this later at the end of the chapter reflection.

Core values are also the foundation of my relentless pursuit of greater results for myself and others. My Results driven values and principles include:

→ Believing every human has been gifted with a unique maximum potential.

→ Law of the O.A.R. - Ownership and Accountability drive Results!

→ A growth mindset focused on continuous improvement and intentional progress.

→ We are called to excellence, not mediocrity or average.

→ Daily habits compounded over time build better results.

→ Progress over perfection.

→ Consistency is the cornerstone of growth.

→ Master self-discipline and remain fiercely consistent.

→ Prioritize your pursuit of greater results with your calendar and finances.

→ Leaders live it and teach others how to multiply results in their lives.

Let me share a couple of "frameworks" that capture many of these values and principles. If leaders implement these behaviors, results will soar! The first framework is the "coaching model," created by Bob Koenig, built upon 4 key leadership behaviors.

→ **Engagement**: We've spent time in a previous chapter discussing and realizing a deeper understanding of the importance of leadership engagement in our own lives first and in the lives of our people and organization. Full engagement is required, all in, 100% of your best daily to drive results upward and onward for your life and for those you love, serve, and lead. Remember the 4 dimensions of our lives: physically, emotionally, mentally, and spiritually. To reach greater levels of our potential and maximize our performance, we must be intentional in every dimension. Remember the "wheel of life" exercise. Implement a growth plan in every dimension of your life. This is the starting point for driving greater results. As a collegiate athlete at Baylor, I can still remember our strength coach reminding us to get 1% every day. We charted it. We tested it. We had to prove it! I think about it in my spiritual walk. I'm mindful of this in my marriage. I can see the faces of the teammates I serve and lead. This commitment to greater results has to be so much more than a checkbox, it has to be lived out and produced for it to matter. Pay the price, it's worth it. Those you lead will be better for it.

→ **High expectations** and goals reflect the core belief that everyone has great potential. As a leader, call your people to the next level. Set goals that honor and stretch your team. Establish clarity around the hopes and goals you have for your organization. Communicate them continuously. Don't leave them undefined. You've heard it said, "People perish without a vision." Invite people on the adventure to higher ground. Have something to shoot for that gets people pumped up and excited. Again, excellence over mediocrity. Stretch beyond your comfort zone.

→ **Create consistent and fierce accountabilities** in your own life and in your leadership with others. Remember, accountability is simply measuring where you are in relation to your goals. Knowing this allows you to reinforce progress while making course adjustments and corrections when off track. it's an opportunity to come beside people, giving them the right amount of support and correction. Remember, we can only give what we have and teach what we know. Accountability starts within your own life and leadership. We have to know the reality of where we truly are and stand with people, relationships, and our performance. I believe strongly in an "inner circle" of people who love you enough to tell you the truth. Iron sharpens iron. I think of my friends who I know I can call anytime, anywhere. When I smell smoke in my life, I call for help. There's freedom in accountability. It helps eliminate blind spots. Why would we not put this into practice in our lives? Pride? Remember the power and posture of humility. It takes time and commitment to build a strong inner circle. Start today if you don't have one!

→ *Master the art of feedback!* It's the game changer of leadership behaviors. It's the one tool we can control to influence behavior change in others. We reinforce the behaviors we want to continue, and we correct those we want to change. You know, leaders are often like parents in the workplace. We have the privilege and responsibility of managing the behaviors of others. We reinforce good behavior while correcting bad behavior. Like all leadership behaviors, we must first learn it, then live it, then teach it! As humble leaders, we embrace the power of feedback in our own lives. As humble leaders, we use feedback to affirm and also lovingly correct our people. On countless occasions, I hear leaders describe the challenge and pain of needing to "deal with" a problem with an employee. Typically, it's been going on for a while. The leader is either afraid to rock the boat or just simply has been ignoring the issue, but now it's risen to a crisis or critical matter. For me, it's an opportunity to let feedback do its magic and transformational work within people. I often remind people of the truth of "deal with the pile while it's small!" We all have piles in our life and leadership to deal with. Feedback sooner than later can help us deal with issues in a positive manner, oftentimes having to pay less now than later if we ignore it. In a culture and relationship committed to giving and receiving feedback, there is freedom to risk, grow, fail, and continue forward. Have the hard conversations you know you need to have today, not tomorrow.

Remember, the heart of feedback is to lovingly support or help someone develop and grow. My motto about feedback is, "If you love me, you'll tell me the truth, good or bad." Consider trying this on in your life and leadership. If you do, you'll see an immediate impact. Feedback sets us free to produce even greater results.

If you master these 4 key leadership behaviors, **RESULTS** will SOAR in your life, leadership, and organization.

The second framework is the *"5 Ps: a Recipe for Abundant Living."* I hope this resonates with you. The foundational belief is that if we ALIGN and consistently live out the following "Ps," we'll drive excellent results in our lives and for those we love, serve, and lead.

→ **PURPOSE**: We've each been created for a specific mission on planet Earth, given unique talents, gifts, and abilities to help make life better for those we love, serve, and lead. It's the "why" of our lives. It's the call we answer. It's the reason we do what we do. It's the inspiration within that ignites the next "P"!

→ **PASSION**: When we know our purpose and pursue it wholeheartedly, it's hard to contain the passion we feel. People see it, feel it, and are oftentimes inspired by it too. It's the "get to" mission our feet get happy to perform. Our heart's purpose is often the "song in our heart" that people can hear. I don't think you can fake a passion. It wells up from within, centered on our purpose, and expresses itself outwardly. It's the energy we feel, even when we're tired, to keep going. For those who don't have clarity about their purpose, it's often something they desire and sometimes become jealous of. You know when you've met someone with passion. It impacts you.

→ **PLAN**: Once we are clear on our purpose and our passion is ignited, we direct our lives with a plan. We align our purpose, passion, and plans with intention. It's one thing to have incredible dreams and hopes, but without a way to implement them in meaningful ways, you fall short of the impact for which they were given to you in the first place. Plans help coordinate and direct a pathway forward. Instead of being blown and tossed around by the emotions of life, we set clear steps and goals to help us unleash our passionate purpose in a productive way! Plans don't eliminate the power and fun of spontaneity but give us a greater opportunity for the completion of the critical tasks at hand.

One of my favorite examples of a leader mastering the ability to plan is the story of Nehemiah in the Bible. He had many leadership traits for us to learn from, but his ability to manage people in executing the rebuilding of the Temple is astounding. Through humble and consistent leadership, He was able to motivate people to complete the daunting task at hand. Nehemiah knew how to implement and execute a plan.

Another proven planning tool to help us build and implement quality plans is the **SMART Goal Model**. It's attributed to Peter Drucker's "Management by Objective" concepts. It's not new and certainly not rocket science. I'm sure you've heard of it, and many of you are probably masters of it. We'll provide a resource for you at the end of the book. For those of you who don't know what it is, or maybe for those of you who need a fresh reminder, here are the basics of the SMART goal strategy:

S - Be specific in your objectives and next steps. Be sure you have clarity and specificity on what the action steps are in your plan. Keep it simple, sensible, and significant.

M - Be sure the goals are meaningful, measurable, and motivating. High expectations, not low. Stretch goals, don't shoot for the comfort zone.

A - Be sure the goals are achievable. Be sure the team and owners of the goals agree on them. Challenged but attainable.

R - Be sure the goals are relevant. Align them with your mission, core values, and capacity. Reasonable and results-driven.

T - Be sure to establish a clear timeline for implementation and completion. Consider the costs of time and resources. Create a sense of urgency.

I find the "project management" process works very well using the SMART goal framework and by implementing the "coaching model" leadership behaviors I've shared with you: engagement, expectations, accountability, and feedback, which directly drive greater results! Integrate and implement these two frameworks, and your results will soar!

Let's get back to the "5 Ps." The next one is:

→ **PRIORITIZE**: Once we've established a plan for our goals, or what I like to call "hopes," powered by our purpose, with contagious passion, we must put our money where our mouth is! We must back our goals with prioritized actions and resources. How many times do we say, or have you heard someone say, "That's a priority for me"? How many of those times is there no action taken? If something is truly a priority for us, that goal is then "set apart" from the others. You can't have more than one top priority. There's only one 1st place, everything else falls in order behind number 1. I'm a big believer in having fewer goals than a long list. I believe in ordering your top 2-3 priorities and making those your life's most important task at hand. So, name your top priorities, and get after them. If your priorities are aligned with your purpose, passion, and plan and actually show up in your calendar and financials as a reflection of how you spend your time and treasure, then get ready for your RESULTS to SOAR! Another thing to remember about priorities. As a leader, it's critical that we teach these principles, like "prioritizing," to our team. You've heard of the Pareto Principle, right? It's the 80/20 rule. 20% of the people do 80% of the work. Frankly, I believe it's shifted more to a 90/10 rule! 10% of the people doing 90% of the work. More on that at another time! My challenge to each of us as leaders is to also prioritize our most important tasks and responsibilities in our work. What if we as leaders truly disciplined ourselves to focus 90% of our time and energy on our top 10% priorities as a CEO, executive leader, etc.? What if we also taught our people and teams this same principle? Just think, an entire team and organization focused on their top priorities! What sort of impact would that create? Would you be able to see a return on that investment of time and resources? I think YES! So, in principle and practice, be sure to invest the time and resources that truly reflect your top priorities. And if you do, you'll experience the final "P" in this recipe for results.

→ **PRODUCTIVITY** drives **RESULTS!** When our passion, purpose, plans, and priorities are aligned and relentlessly pursued, incredible productivity, progress, and RESULTS are attained! Enough said. The proof is in the outcomes. Try the recipe. You will not be disappointed!

So, you've been reminded of and learned a few new perspectives, tools, and realities about results. I hope you've caught a new strategy or framework to help you strengthen your approach and achievement of results in your life and leadership. Remember, once you catch it, be sure to teach it to your family and teams. Keep your O.A.R. (ownership, accountability, results) front of mind throughout the process. Be SMART. Follow the 5 Ps recipe for success. Be intentional. Be 1% better every day. Today is the day... So, let's GO!!!

End of Chapter Questions- Results (Read Colossians 3:23)

1. What areas of your life and leadership do you consider the principle and responsibility of stewardship? How does it show up in your life and leadership?

2. How do you measure success? Are you more progress or perfection focused on your expectations of yourself? Others?

3. How do you practice accountability in your life and leadership? How can you increase accountability with your team?

4. What aspects of feedback are easy for you to practice? Which are difficult for you and why?

5. List daily habits you have mastered that drive positive results in your life. Consider all four dimensions of your life. Where do you have room to grow? Are there any habits you need to release?

CHAPTER 6

Today Matters!

Friends, I hope you're enjoying the journey of this book through the Leadership H.E.A.R.T. But if our time together only reaches a level of enjoyment without deep introspection and conviction, resulting in a new commitment to grow and strengthen every dimension of your life and leadership, then I've fallen short of the hope and purpose of this book. I truly began this process to encourage, equip, and empower you to lift your leadership performance in all dimensions of your life. I want to lift your peak performance to new heights. Unless this book stirs your heart and soul into action and makes you want to grow your life and leadership, I've not been a very good communicator and influencer in your life.

But if even a spark of desire or hunger for more has been stirred within your heart, let's keep going! There is incredible purpose and power within you, grounded in a high calling to live, love, serve, and lead with excellence and impact. There's hero stuff within you. I dare you to unleash it. We all have room to grow and get better. Not tomorrow. Not another time. But right now. Yes, right now. Today. Not someday. Remember, *SOMEDAY IS TODAY!*

Let me look you square in the eyes and challenge you to embrace the gift and opportunity of every day we are blessed to experience and live. TODAY matters! Stop and consider if you truly believe this truth. Does today really matter to you? Talk and head nodding are cheap unless it's real, from the depths of your heart and soul, compelling you to action. It's tragic to me that so many times, we think it's ok to put things off until tomorrow or some other day. Another time, but not now. Let me say it again… ***SOMEDAY IS TODAY!***

Let's become part of the "priceless few" who launch out into the deep waters of growth and abundant life, never giving up on reaching new heights and depths of their potential. The "priceless few" make up about 1% of the population. About 4-5% reach leadership levels, with the remaining 95% of the masses being content to go along their own way of comfort and status quo. Good is good enough for over 95% of the people walking around planet Earth. Is that the greatest hope and trajectory of your life and leadership? Not for me, and I'm hearing you say, "Not for me either!" It takes everything we've shared together in this book so far—Humility, Full Engagement, Attitude, Results driven habits and mindset, and last but not least, embracing the incredible opportunity given to us TODAY.

I'm realizing, too, as a 50+ adult, there is truly no guarantee of tomorrow. Frankly, today and maybe the next few hours are all I have to live, love, serve, and lead. We all know life happens, and within seconds, our lives can be disrupted by so many things out of our control and oftentimes by things we've never thought of happening. Tragic and sudden deaths of loved ones and friends. Diagnosis and test results. Loss of a job. The list goes on and on and on. This reality of life is just that, a part of living human life on earth. Even as a person of faith as my life's anchor, which gives me great peace amidst these trials, it's not a choice for me to become content or passive today. It spurs me on to an even greater desire to live life to its fullest.

You've heard the phrase "carpe diem." This charge is used to urge someone to make the most of the present time and give little thought to the future. I agree with the first part of the definition but not the later part. Yes, give your all today, with tomorrow and the future in mind! What we do matters tomorrow. Here's another way I think about the hope and potential given to us every day. Our finish line today, in what we start, move forward, or even complete, is the new starting line for tomorrow. Everyday compounds on the next. We repeat this rhythm every day.

Now, let me stop here and remind us of a very important truth we discussed in our "full engagement" chapter. The opportunity, and frankly responsibility, to get started today by giving our 100% in every dimension doesn't negate the responsibility of taking time to rest, recover, recharge, and repeat! Remember the examples the athletes give us. Every day they're either preparing, performing, or recovering. Remember the formula? It's 90% preparation, 10% performance. This is followed without fail with a very intentional time to rest, heal, and recover. So, as we answer the call to make the very most out of every day, we must be disciplined to include days of rest and recovery. Got it? Even the creator of this incredible world took a day to rest. So did His Son. So can we.

Because TODAY MATTERS, let's get started! Consider where you are on your leadership journey. For some, you're truly on the initial starting line of becoming a leader. For some, who have experience in a variety of leadership roles, it's a matter of being reminded and sharpening the tools necessary to keep growing and getting better. For others, you've truly mastered a high level of leadership, and it's a season for you to truly pour into developing others. Whatever your location is on the journey, your starting line is today. Here's a short quote that drives the importance of starting today from Nike founder Phil Knight, "The cowards never started, and the weak died along the way." Only the strong start and come through! So let's GO!

Let's review a passage from scripture that deals with time and the importance of today. It's found in Ecclesiastes 3:1-8. I'm sure you're familiar with this passage, often titled "A Time for Everything." I'm curious if you find any leadership principles or truths in this passage. I've shared a few reflections and key learnings for me in this passage below.

Ecclesiastes 3:1-8 "A Time for Everything" (English Standard Version)

1. *"There is a time for everything and a season for every activity under the heavens."*

Leadership truth and reflections: Every day matters, and there is value in every season we walk through

2. *"A time to be born and a time to die, a time to plant and a time to uproot."*

Leadership truth and reflections: As leaders, there is a time when we begin, grow, develop, peak, multiply and develop others, and end our time. Sometimes we adjust and change, maybe voluntarily or involuntarily. Our role, position, and influence are not a given, it's cyclical.

3. *"A time to kill and a time to heal, a time to tear down and a time to build."*

Leadership truth and reflections: While we don't ever encourage "killing" anyone, of course, there are times when we cause things to cease—relationships, habits, behaviors, and terminations.

Side note: I believe people "fire" themselves, and leaders have the responsibility to manage the process with dignity and clarity. Leaders are hope givers, and through example, we initiate forgiveness and reconciliation within our own lives, families, and workplaces. We tear down walls and silos, and we build trust and teams. We discontinue a service or product line and replace it with something better and more relevant.

4. *"A time to weep and a time to laugh, a time to mourn and a time to dance."*

<u>Leadership truth and reflections</u>: Leaders have the incredible privilege of walking beside their people in good times and sometimes in very dark, tough places of grief and loss. We can also share joy and celebrations with our people. Humble leaders are transparent and compassionate, willing to meet people where they are, and yes, sometimes even willing to celebrate out loud and have fun!

5. *"A time to scatter stones and a time to gather them, a time to embrace and a time to refrain from embracing."*

<u>Leadership truths and reflections</u>: Change is inevitable, and sometimes we are the change agents. Sometimes we receive someone with compassion and grace and extend a second chance. Sometimes we draw the line and separate.

6. *"A time to search and a time to give up, a time to keep and a time to throw away."*

<u>Leadership truths and reflections:</u> we constantly seek growth and improvement, looking for better. Sometimes we give up on the current path by redirecting our focus and energy to a different path. Loyalty and tenure can be great traits, maintaining continuity, but there are also times to bring in fresh water and new people, ideas, and strategies.

7. *"A time to tear and a time to mend, a time to be silent and a time to speak."*

<u>Leadership truths and reflections:</u> there are times to confront and times to reconcile. Absolutely there are times to listen and times to speak. I'm

reminded of James—quick to listen, slow to speak, slow to anger. Great leadership advice!

8 *"A time to love and a time to hate, a time for war and a time for peace."*

<u>Leadership truths and reflections</u>: Always love in action, even when giving discipline or correction. Always "hate" lying, stealing, disrespect, misaligned values, toxic thinking, and behavior. Leaders are defenders of their mission, values, and people, standing against anything that threatens or tries to harm them. Leaders are peacemakers internally, resolving conflict and differences respectfully and directly. Leaders seek unity and alignment with core values at every level within the organization. Leaders fight negative self-talk and replace it with positive self-talk.

How did you enjoy that walk through Ecclesiastes? Did you catch other leadership principles or truths? You'll have a chance to write these down at the end of this chapter. I'd love to hear them!

Let me share a few other leadership principles and truths I believe help us embrace the gift and opportunity of TODAY. First, I believe in the power of process. Our best is not developed in a day. Leadership develops daily. Every single day, we have the opportunity to move our life and leadership upward and onward to greater levels of growth and performance. The same is true for those we love, serve, and lead. In other words, our growth is not a static state. It's dynamic. As leaders, we must learn to trust the process. The really good news is that no matter where we are starting from or performing today, we can all grow and get better. I think we can all agree that living and leading can be very complicated. At least it is for me! Just think about the four dimensions of our life and leadership we've considered in this book. It's complex. It has so many facets. It reminds us that leadership growth and development in all four dimensions take time. For those of you who enjoy cooking, especially grilling (my favorite), a really good end result often involves the perfect seasoning and marinating, both of which take time and, if done well, turn into a really good-tasting outcome. As leaders, we require this same sequence of seasoning to be most effective.

Another aspect of the process is the compounding power of our daily agenda and habits. If we truly align our life and leadership with the principles and power of the Leadership H.E.A.R.T., we will see inevitable growth over time. Growth and maximum performance is a long game. It's a "long road of obedience" to the principles we've discussed.

So, let me encourage you to consider and remember the following truths about the process, all of which we've studied in this book:

→ It takes time to grow and mature. Like competitive athletes, spend the time and do the work to prepare. Stay faithful in the daily grind. Live and learn these principles, giving you the platform to teach and multiply these principles in the lives of those you love, serve, and lead. Be patiently persistent!

→ Gold is purified after it's passed repeatedly through intense heat and fire. We, too, are like precious metals—like gold—and are refined in the same way. Remember to embrace the trials and challenges that WILL come your way. Stay the course, even under pressure. It's often at these critical crisis moments our true colors show, and our leadership matters most. Ask for help and support as needed but stay the course to completion.

> → Stay true and aligned with your core values. These become pillars and nonnegotiables in your life and leadership. For me, it's built on the foundation of my faith and relationship with Jesus. It's my anchor. Find your faith anchor and build your life and leadership on its values and truths.

Another important truth about TODAY, and our trajectory to grow and develop our leadership, involves mastering the concept of "timing." Timing is critical in making good decisions and better ones. My favorite way to describe the power of timing is through a baseball analogy I witnessed and experienced multiple times in my career, on and off the field: Timing is the difference between a long foul ball and a home run! Think about it. If the batter swings early, even if it's solid contact with the ball, it flies over the fence in foul territory. Not counting or changing the score. But if a batter has really good timing, the contact between the bat and the ball results in a home run, changing the score and counting!

Mastering the principle of "timing" is so important and really challenging to do. It involves the balance of having enough information to make a decision or sometimes having enough faith to take a risk and go for it. Do you have the gift of timing in your life and leadership? If you do, way to go! Please teach the rest of us.

Here are some things to remember when you're making decisions that require the right timing:

> → Stay focused on the big picture, staying in close proximity (engagement) with your people, mission, and priorities. Keeping a consistent pulse on things gives you greater discernment when a

prime opportunity presents itself, allowing you to take the initiative and seize the prize at the right time. I'm not a huge believer in coincidence. I believe in God's plan for my life and in the power of staying engaged with your people and mission. It's an intentional discipline with great dividends.

→ Test your decisions by engaging key people in the process with you. Listen, ask questions, and consider how the opportunity aligns with your mission, values, and people. Include the front lines when appropriate. Our front line people oftentimes know the realities of our world of work better than we do as leaders. Again, stay engaged all the way to the front lines.

→ In leadership and life, there's really no such thing as "zero risk." Consider the cost and benefits for all involved. Measure the risk with potential payoff. Seek buy-in from your team, but also be willing to go alone if you feel deep conviction it's the right thing to do. Know that sometimes you'll make the right call, at the right time, with the right outcome. know too that there will be times we miss it too. The victories build momentum, and any failures can be great learning opportunities if we allow them to teach us.

TODAY gives us the opportunity to build momentum in our lives and leadership. Momentum can be a leader's best friend! To build momentum we know there has to be a starting point. Once we commit to the DAILY GRIND, with very intentional actions aligned with our purpose/mission, aligned with our values, set apart as priorities, implemented through strategic activities, the "Big Mo" begins!

Think of a time in your life and leadership you felt the power of momentum. For me, it's right now. As my life and leadership story continues to evolve, the commitment I made two years ago to get right in all dimensions of my life and leadership (fully engaged), starting to compete in powerlifting meets, has truly caused Big Mo to continue even today, including serving as a catalyst for me to share my Leadership H.E.A.R.T. book with you! It took commitment and resolve, followed by relentless daily actions aligned with my values and promises to myself, my wife, my daughter and coach, and to all those I love, serve, and lead. I feel like I'm just getting started. What about you?

Let's consider some momentum builders and potential momentum blockers:

Builders:	Blockers:
Maximizing TODAY!	Someday mindset
Cultural values	Misaligned people and purpose
Faith	Fear
Starting	Procrastination
Empowering self-talk	Self-limiting beliefs
Teamwork	Isolation
Inner circle of support/challenge	Arrogance/pride
Progress and results	Stagnation
Daily habits/discipline	Impulsivity
Consistency	inconsistency
Failing forward	Ignoring the lessons
Passionate purpose	No purpose, no passion
Victory	Defeat/quitting

Full "O.A.R."	
(Ownership, Accountability, Results)	BLAMING OTHERS
Leading by example	Hypocrisy
Alignment to values/mission	No vision, direction, common ground
Intentional leadership transition plans	No succession plans
Leadership trust and credibility	Boss holes reign/toxic culture

So, based on this list of builders and blockers, how would you describe the momentum in your life and leadership? Is it increasing? What's blocking your momentum?

Well, we've looked at multiple aspects of the impact on leadership and the power and potential of TODAY! Do you feel any different now than you did when you began this chapter? Do we need to get "eye to eye" again and assess your level of excitement and resolve to pursue the deepest waters of living and leading at your very best? My hope is you're fired up and ready to **GROW!** I invite you to join me TODAY on this incredible adventure and opportunity to truly change the world for those you love, serve, and lead. And remember, it starts within YOU! I dare you to launch out and unleash your leadership H.E.A.R.T., igniting your revolution of influence and impact TODAY!

End of Chapter Questions- Today (Read Joshua 24:15-17)

1. How would you describe the value you put on "today"? Are there any habits or decisions you're putting off for "someday"? If so, choose one to begin working on today!

2. What leadership truths or principles do you see in the Ecclesiastes passage we read? How can you implement these into your life and leadership today?

3. How well do you "trust the process" as a leader? What can sometimes cause you to interrupt the process for you or your team? What one truth about "process" resonated with you today that you will begin implementing in your life and leadership?

4. How would you rate the level of momentum in your life? Leadership? Marriage? Which dimensions of your life do you feel like you have momentum? What's blocking momentum in the other dimensions? What momentum "blockers" do you need to deal with first?

5. Consider seeking feedback from your team, family, or inner circle on how people view your momentum "builders" vs. "blockers." Stay humble and receive the feedback. Create an action plan where needed. Challenge your team, family, and inner circle to do the same!

CHAPTER 7

Closing - From My Heart to Yours

As we conclude this learning journey together, my hope is that you've learned new insights about leading yourself and others. You've been reminded of essential core and fundamental truths and principles about leadership and personal growth. You've discovered new ideas and applications for raising your leadership performance and influence on new levels of impact and influence. I've likely learned more than you in this process of writing and sharing my Leadership H.E.A.R.T. The choice is yours on how you respond to the leadership truths in this book. The next steps are in your court. Remember, there is no finish line to growth, and your very best is yet to come. So, how do we wrap up this learning experience together?

From my heart to yours, it's only right for me to leave you with a final "charge." Regardless of your faith and beliefs, a charge applies to every leader. The word "charge" implies a divine, constant, compelling, lifetime command to all leaders, ministers, workers, disciples, and followers of the Lord to continue in the sound doctrine of the word of God and the leadership truths and principles it so clearly teaches. A charge is a duty and responsibility that must be obeyed. When these principles and truths are followed, great results occur. There is growth and transformation within the leader, and for those being loved, served, and led.

Friend, will you answer my final charge to you as a leader?

→ *I DARE YOU* to own the very unique gifts, talents, experiences, and strengths you possess as a leader, spouse, parent, and friend.

→ *I DARE YOU* to create accountabilities in all dimensions of your life and leadership and always pursue the truth of your realities and opportunities.

→ *I DARE YOU* to commit to a growth mindset, releasing anything or anyone holding you back from your very best, relentlessly pursuing your new habits and future state daily.

→ *I DARE YOU* to unleash your purpose and passion at home, work, and play so people can see, hear, and feel the freedom and life-giving love you have for those you love, serve and lead.

→ *I DARE YOU* to stay close to your mission, people, and priorities. Commit to full engagement in every dimension of your life, no matter how big or small the cost.

→ *I DARE YOU* to be a multiplier, *NOT* a divider. Learn it, live it, and then teach these principles and truths to the people you love, serve, and lead.

→ *I DOUBLE DOG DARE YOU* to *NOT* be a "boss-hole," but be a leader with H.E.A.R.T. Discover your own core values as a leader. Champion them daily for yourself and for those you lead. And don't ever forget: *your leadership matters!*

My hope and prayer are that all seven of these "charges" will be lived out in your life and leadership beginning today. Even if you choose only one of these to embrace, your life and leadership will be better for it. And remember, when you teach others to live and lead this way, the multiplication impact of these truths affects everything in your team, family, and organization. ***Will you answer this call?***

Friends, unleash your leadership **H.E.A.R.T.,** igniting a revolution of influence and impact in your life and leadership TODAY!

Lead on!

Chad Patterson

Leader,

If you've found any value or benefit to your life and leadership from the truths and principles of this book, feel free to let me know! I would love to hear your key learnings and priority next steps. If I can add any value to your life and leadership, please connect with me to discuss the solutions and services I can deliver to you, your team, and your organization.

Connect with Chad today at www.chadpattersoncoaching.com

Follow Chad on Social Media at:
www.linkedin.com/in/chadlpatterson
www.facebook.com/chadpattersoncoaching

Chad Patterson Coaching delivers the following core services:
Leadership Coaching
Keynote Speaking
Leadership Development Training & Curriculum
Accountable Leader Program
Leadership Retreats & Conferences

RESOURCES: Core Leadership Frameworks & Principles

1. "3 things Leaders are called to do": (Intro Chapter)

1. Champion Core Values (walking, living billboard, and picture)
2. Develop people (including themselves)
3. Drive results! (taking people from their current state to a better future state!)

2. Leaders take people from Here (current state) to There (future) (Introduction)

THERE (Future state) The goals, targets, hopes we are pursuing.

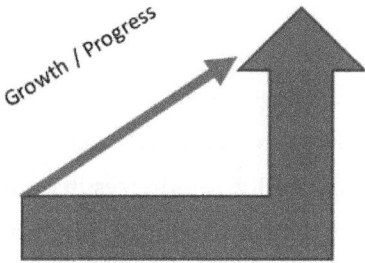

HERE ("Current State") Where we are today.

3. Leadership Coaching Module: (Results Chapter)

(Created by Bob Koenig, adapted by Chad Patterson)

1. Foundation: commitment/proximity to people & mission
2. Goals/Hopes/Targets
3. Accountability measures
4. Feedback (confirmation/correction)
5. These leadership behaviors DRIVE RESULTS!

The key to success is a leader implementing these in their own lives, then teaching/multiplying these behaviors in leaders at every level of their org.

4. The "Leadership Multiplication Effect" (Heart chapter)

Jesus lived and taught his values to his disciples. He grew them and sent them out to "multiply" those leadership truths, values, and behaviors, and the process continues today. As leaders, we have the same opportunity to live out our values, teaching them to others and developing them to take the principles and behaviors to the organization's front lines. It allows for the "3 things leaders are called to do" to be multiplied through leadership at every level. This aligns with core values throughout the entire organization.

5." Law of the Hoola Hoop" – (Engagement Chapter)

a human behavior theory called "Locus of Control," aka "The O.A.R." Principle: We have the choice to have an internal locus of control, which takes full ownership, accountability, and active responsibility for the results and consequences of our actions. Or, to have an external locus of control, where all of the ownership, accountability, and responsibility for results and consequences is given away to everyone but me, oftentimes referred to as a "victim's mindset."

Strong and effective leaders commit to full ownership of their lives, accountability for their choices, and are fully responsible for their life results.

1. Internal locus of control fully follows the OAR.
2. External locus of control puts OAR on everyone else but themselves, "victim" mindset

6. Recipe for Abundant Living: 5 Ps-Purpose, Passion, Plan, Priority, Produce results! (Results Chapter)

If we align these Ps in our lives, it creates maximum performance and abundant joy!

7. The 3Rs Coaching Technique: Release, Reach, Remain (Engagement Chapter)

- Release mindsets, people, habits that keep you from being your very best, holding you back.

- Reach for new mindsets, habits, people, and goals that build you up and move you forward.

- Remain in the new habits, mindsets, and relationships, making the new growth nonnegotiable.

REPEAT this process over and over for the rest of your life!

8. Wheel of Life Exercise (Engagement Chapter)

Identify areas of your life to increase your engagement and growth.

9. S.M.A.R.T. Goal Strategy (Results Chapter)

S: Specific

M: Measurable

A: Attainable

R: Relevant and results-driven

T: Timelines for implementation and completion

SPECIAL NOTE:

Chad Patterson Coaching/I am committing proceeds from the sales of my book to a ministry initiative at our church called "The Oasis Project". The Oasis Project is a plan by Mobberly Baptist Church in Longview, TX to use its nearly 140-acre campus to develop an "oasis in the woods" to minister to and bless hurting people, including pastors, missionaries, married couples, and others who are broken, burned-out, and need healing.

Please learn more at www.mobberly.org/oasis

Lead on!

Chad Patterson, Founder and Coach

Chad Patterson Coaching

www.chadpattersoncoaching.com

210-562-0013

"Leadership Affects Everything!"

THANK YOU FOR READING MY BOOK!

CLAIM YOUR FREE WELCOME CALL

Just to say thanks for buying and reading my book, I would like to give you a free welcome call with me, no strings attached!

I appreciate your interest in my book, and value your feedback as it helps me improve future versions. I would appreciate it if you could leave your invaluable review on Amazon.com with your feedback. Thank you!

www.ingramcontent.com/pod-product-compliance
Lightning Source LLC
LaVergne TN
LVHW011429080426
835512LV00005B/348